Jan. 2021

Maria

Happy New Year!
I SAW THIS AT AN ANTIQUE
STORE IN NEW ORLEANS &
THOUGHT you WOULD LOVE IT!
HOPE you'RE WELL !

love.
Cousin Andrew
Kasprzycki

*New Orleans' Napoleon House is a Mecca for civilized drinking,
a Waterloo for thirst . . .*

. . . One look and you know you'll be getting one mother of a civilized drink.
Beth Arnold, Gentleman's Quarterly, *December 1992*

Book and jacket design: Kerri McCaffety and Cynthia McCaffety

ISBN 978-0-9709336-6-9

Library of Congress Control Number: 2006927713

Printed in Korea.

Published for Cheers Publishing L.L.C. by:

Vissi d'Arte Books
P. O. Box 791054
New Orleans, LA 70179

www.vissidartebooks.com

VISSI
D'ARTE

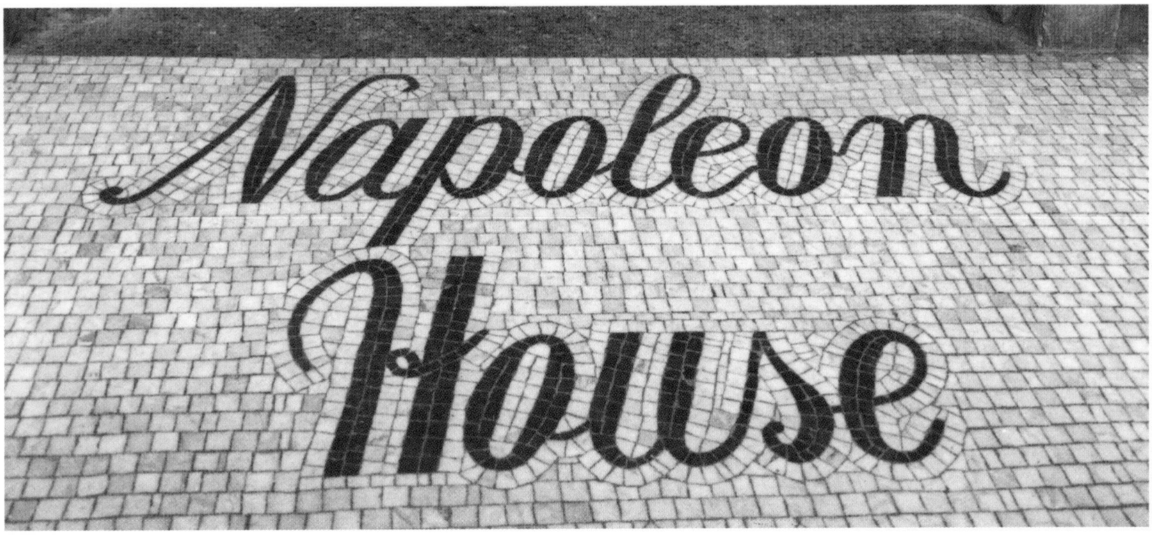
Napoleon
House

Dedicated to the Impastato Family

Contents

There are places for afternoon and early evening like the Napoleon House, where in the carefully maintained decay, locals can impress out-of-towners with the size of the roaches and the melancholy of a vivid and shadowy past. Napoleon could have lived here, if he hadn't died, but the implication is that he does live here, upstairs perhaps, and that he might descend the curved staircase any time to join the conversation.

— Andrei Codrescu
excerpt from the introduction to Obituary Cocktail

introduction

portraits of a legend

Pictures crowd the walls of the Napoleon House. The sheer number of them is one of its subliminally overwhelming features as you sit underneath their stare, their stature, and their stories. Each image allows a teasing glimpse at a fascinating history. A book could be written about any single tale of any single painting. Many have been.

Of course, there are the portraits of *him*. The entire life of *him* can be traced in the time it takes to eat the spicy okra out of your Bloody Mary: Napoleon as young general, Napoleon's coronation, Napoleon's victory at Austerlitz, Napoleon I in his study, Napoleon's divorce, Napoleon's exile. One liquor company cleverly enlarged David's Napoleon Crossing the Alps into a poster capturing only the intense glare of a hyper-motivated genius or driven despot, depending on your politics. This poster glowers over you as you sit in the calm inner room having "Just a bowl of gumbo, please." With the General looking at you like that, it makes you feel like you should order more.

Also on the walls are the hagiographic descriptions of the Napoleon House itself from the world's journals. Carefully preserved in glass and wood, the stories focus on the singular grace of the bistro, and the singular family stories of the dynasty that runs it. Mixed in with the news articles on the walls are moving images of the forebears—Nicholas Girod looking a bit like the French version of Mr. Bennet from Pride and Prejudice, kindly, loving, but philosophically aloof; "Uncle Joe" Impastato, progenitor of the modern business, romantically captured in a series of photos by Louis Sahuc. One arresting sepia-toned photograph has avuncular Old Joe, at least 90, seated with his cane and a smile, and a six-shooter shoved in his belt. A painted portrait of the classy Peter Impastato has his chin confidently lifted up against Napoleon on his horse, arrogantly returning the look. The two images bookending a wall prompts you to wonder who is the international celebrity, and who is the family hero. In this place, is there a difference?

And among these prolific icons scattered Louvre-like upon the walls, sometimes five high, are some not-so-inspiring works: standard still lifes possibly the efforts of some early family member's flirtation with art class. These fruit-and-wine-bottle projects are of the type found in any Italian restaurant in America. You know the type. Usually the sort of place your dad would take the family when mom didn't want to cook on a Sunday. Remember? One Coke. "You get one Coke to drink for the meal, and you better save it, 'cuz that's it." And while nursing the precious soda, you would sullenly pick at your antipasto, your gnocchis, and if mom made a stand, your spumoni. And you wouldn't realize how exquisite the meal was until you got to college and tried to make spaghetti and sauce for the first time.

Because despite the international reputation, the close association with the history of the most historic city in America, despite even the perfection of its antique condition, the Napoleon House above all is what some folks would call "a family place." The kids can go sit in the courtyard with grandma and eat antipasto, while mom and dad go into the bar for a cognac, just like the Italian restaurants of your youth.

The walls of the Napoleon House reflect a subconscious and not so sublime identification with greatness and familial devotion. It is interesting that Napoleon parceled all his striving and passions among his own family. And when you come to the end of your Bloody Mary, surrounded by the faces and places on the walls of everyone and everywhere important to the generations of owners, you might feel you yourself have been iconized into a tableau containing the latest members of the Napoleon House family.

I grew up hearing my father's stories about his bachelor apartment in the Napoleon House. His roommate was a lawyer who defended bootleggers, so they always had lots to drink and gave parties. He told me he kept a pet boa constrictor in the apartment and would let it out to run occasionally.

—Marcelle d'Aquin Saussy
New Orleans native

the plot
to rescue the Emperor

No discussion about 500 rue Chartres proceeds without broaching the subject of The Plot. Every carriage driver who clip-clops by, every airline magazine article, and of course, the restaurant menu itself, all relate the tale of how civic leaders and hardened pirates met to free the great Napoleon Bonaparte from his exile and give him this house as a home.

Addressing the issues around The Plot is quite like trying to explain that December 31, 1999, was *not* the last day of the millennium: one could pull out all the math books, calendars, and ephemerides possible while a disenchanted audience rolls its eyes and patiently listens—then, guess what? The world partied in 1999, while New Year's Eve 2000 had a much less prolific send-off. The idea that a bunch of French patriots met in a foggy tavern, at the heart of a legendary town, to undertake a mission that was at once swashbuckling, noble, and world-changing makes so much intuitive sense—like a sensible ending to the millennium—that if isn't true, it ought to be.

Naturally, many iterations to the story exist. The most common claims the news of the Emperor's exile so inflamed the local *Bonapartistas*, that the mayor brought together a junta of money, men, and sailors. The buccaneers would sneak out in a fast ship, run to St. Helena, evade the naval patrols, climb up the rocky cliffs, overpower the guards, strap *l'Empereur* to a chair, lower him to the craft, and escape to *la Nouvelle Orléans*. Mayor Nicolas Girod would build a home for Napoleon at the lot he had just inherited from his brother—the present-day Napoleon House. Alas, three days before the ship was to set sail, the tale continues, the sad news of the passing of Bonaparte scuttled the mission.

Different versions elect different captains. Most of the time, the culprit is the elder Captain St. Ange Bossière, famous for his daring attacks on Mexican shores, and who supposedly had a 200-ton schooner named *La Sèraphine*. Some stories have him special-ordering it out of Charleston, South Carolina. A *Daily Picayune* journalist in 1907 arrogantly wrote, "No hair-brained scheme was this impossible of accomplishment," and goes on to describe, without the inconvenience of evidence, how the ship was painted black and its sails dyed with tea to make her undetectable on the midnight seas. Another story nominates Dominique You, a cannoneer from the Napoleonic campaigns in Santo Domingo (Haiti) and renowned filibuster, as the expedition's captain. Still more accounts put none other than Jean Lafitte at the helm.

Adding to the confusion, from the time of a report in Coleman's 1884 *Guide to New Orleans* through World War II, it was in vogue to believe Mayor Girod lived in his own house and built another house, 514 Chartres, as the Imperial Residence. (Coleman cites it as 124 Chartres under the old system of addresses in the Vieux Carré.) For a time, a sign hung on that building proclaiming it as "The Old Napoleon House." Today it is the Pharmacy Museum.

This "tradition that defies substantiation" is a deliciously entrenched story. There is no direct proof for it, and no direct proof against it. The story gets incestuously related and re-related back and forth from guidebooks, newspaper travel sections, tourist fodder, public speeches, and other public records, so not only does it become "fact" by default, it also becomes difficult to extract what, if anything, really happened.

For example, Coleman, after voluptuously describing the rescue plans featuring intricate,

Jean Lafitte

Jean Lafitte at Dominique You's Bar, c. 1830, by John Wesley Jarvis, 1781-1840. Painting supposedly depicts Jean and Pierre Lafitte seated (Jean raising cup), and You standing. Courtesy of the Louisiana State Museum.

The apartments awaiting Napoleon on the second floor of the Napoleon House.

arcane sketches prepared by draughtsmen, and corsairs with sabers in their teeth, goes on to talk about the untimely death of the Emperor: "Alas! alas! alas! Man proposes, God disposes," writes Coleman, "That the plot we have described was known to and authorized by Napoleon's staff was long afterward acknowledged by Dr. Antomarcchi and Marshall Bertrand."

The two men mentioned were members of Napoleon's staff on the island, who finally came to New Orleans. Coleman's report is unencumbered by any compelling proof beyond his own word. Eleven years later, Judge Castellanos, obviously lifting his information from Coleman, writes, "Of this project there can be no doubt," and leaves it at that.

"CAPTIVE."

FROM THE PAINTING BY ALBERT PIERRE DAWANT.

A small print entitled "Captive" hangs in the second-floor apartments.

Just as obviously using these two sources, the Daily Picayune writer in 1907 adds his own proof of the two staffers corroborating the story. Apparently Bertrand had written a letter to Napoleon's brother, Joseph, who was living in Virginia. In the letter he admits to fantasizing about walking in the beautiful hills of Virginia. This proves nothing, as being stuck on a rock halfway between Africa and South America would make cavorting in Virginia seem like a really great alternative. Besides, Joseph was living in New Jersey.

On the one hand, it makes total sense that the types of Creoles living in town at the time, so freshly victorious at the Battle of New Orleans, would feel a bit invincible. A clandestine journey by ship would be easy to accomplish with the resources in the port city. Girod himself had made his fortune as an importer and merchant, and would be in close contact with maritime-types. For example, Girod's business partner, Simon Laignel, gave the eulogy at Dominique You's funeral in 1830.

Also, the establishment of the new (old) regime in France scattered the Republican followers all over the globe, and many of them came to New Orleans. So it would stand to reason any man plucky enough to come to the New World to make a new life would certainly not flinch at such an enterprise as saving his idol and commander-in-chief. And finally, as far as lack of evidence is concerned, it's not as if there could be a headline in the newspaper screaming, "Super-Secret Mission to Steal the Most Important Captive in the World from the Clutches of the Most Powerful Navy in the World Set to Sail Today."

On the other hand, there is no direct, extant evidence of the plot. There are no diary entries, no actual references to the plot from the exiles on St. Helena, no one in New Orleans came forward after Napoleon's death, there is not even a shred of evidence that the *Sèraphine* existed. At Dominique You's funeral, of all the great and scandalous achievements outlined by Laignel, there is no mention of his involvement with The Plot. One would assume, years after Bonaparte's death, it would be a glorious and safe addition to his heroics. It certainly would have played well to the Creoles in attendance. Perhaps, if there were a plot, You was not involved.

GIROD HOUSE
ERECTED IN 1814
BY
NICHOLAS GIROD
THE TWO STORY WING FACING
ST. LOUIS STREET WAS BUILT BY
HIS BROTHER, CLAUDE FRANÇOIS GIROD,
ABOUT 1792.

NICHOLAS GIROD WAS THE MAYOR
OF NEW ORLEANS FROM 1812 TO 1815
AND IT IS SAID THAT HE OFFERED
HIS HOUSE AS A PLACE OF REFUGE
FOR NAPOLEON BONAPARTE IN A
PLOT TO RESCUE HIM FROM EXILE.

So what do we know? Placing the following events on a timeline may provide some insight into The Plot.

- Nicolas Girod was elected the fifth mayor of New Orleans on September 21, 1812. He was re-elected on September 4, 1814.

- On May 4, 1814, Napoleon Bonaparte was exiled to the island of Elba, in the Mediterranean. Because "news services" of the time were whatever dispatches, letters, foreign journals, or personal accounts arriving from wherever they came, New Orleans newspapers had to piece together bits until, three or four months after the fact, a story could be confirmed. The city discovered the exile on July 9 when a French ship came up the river with the news, and an assurance that the king was still interested in trade for the city's many valuable goods.

- Earlier that year, the mayor's brother Claude died, leaving the property to Nicolas. On April 26, 1814, it is recorded that there is a "two story" house with a tile roof on the property. (When the third story was added is another mystery for another time).

- The year 1815 starts miserably for New Orleans, as the weather is sloppier than usual, the British are marching through the swamps toward the city, the locals are sure Andrew Jackson will burn the city rather than lose, and Napoleon is still in exile. However, the Battle of New Orleans concludes successfully for the Americans on January 8, 1815. Girod and You distinguish themselves at the fight.

- Napoleon escapes Elba on March 1, 1815. It comes to the attention of the city on May 23 when the *Louisiana Gazette* (which rarely used one exclamation point) proclaims, "Counter Revolution in France!!"

Arthur, in his 1936 history, without asserting its authenticity, notes an interesting story that has the city fathers at a performance at the St. Phillip Theatre when the news of Napoleon's escape is discovered. Everyone immediately speculates that he will not only come to the United States, but that he will come to New Orleans. Where else? It is easy to imagine the happy shock. "After our victory at Chalmette, and now this, certainly God must be on our side!" In an absolutely believable scenario, the story has Mayor Girod leaping onto the stage to announce that if indeed the Emperor comes to New Orleans, he would give his new house (now only a year old) to him. If there could be any tenable seed to the legend, this proposed event could certainly qualify.

But the year goes downhill for both the mayor and the emperor. On September 4, 1815, Girod resigns his political post because of financial troubles. As for Napoleon, after his so-called "Hundred Days," he disembarks on the second of his island exiles. This time, on October 15, 1815, he is on lonely little *Ste. Hélène*, in the middle of the Atlantic Ocean. It's not clear when New Orleans learns of the second exile, but the March 15, 1816, edition of the *Louisiana Courier* complains that Bonaparte's residence, Longwood, isn't being prepared fast enough; and it gloomily reports, "St. Helena will be secured from any sudden attack that might be projected for the liberation of the prisoner; and as for the means of stealth, it is not likely they can succeed since every caution has been given by the government on this head."

"Fine," a disciple of The Plot might say, "the gauntlet was dropped, the reports of the island's impregnability only spurred the fiercely proud, clever French nationalists on." After all, a few Englishmen couldn't scare them ...

In all the versions of The Plot, there is the cautionary tale-style ending that says, "Just before the expedition was to leave, Napoleon died, and with it, the visionary plan." But in the New Orleans consciousness, when exactly did Napoleon die?

It is well documented that the conqueror of nations died, probably of arsenic poisoning, in captivity on May 5, 1821. Still ignorant of this news Stateside, the *Courier* on August 10, 1821, reports that his condition is fine, but finishes with a disturbing non sequitur: "In case of death his body is ... to be sent to London to satisfy the world that no violence had been inflicted on him."

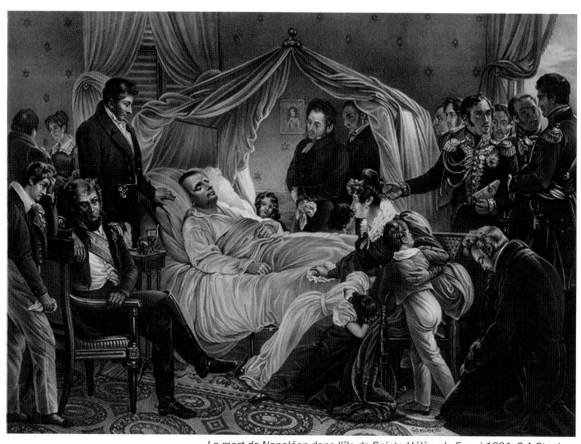

La mort de Napoléon dans l'île de Sainte Hélène le 5 mai 1821, C.A.Steuben

Some histories document that New Orleans learned of Bonaparte's death on his birthday and city holiday, August 15. This is not true. The papers of that day dismiss a report of his death as a "rumor." The *Louisiana Gazette* writes on August 22, "We do not place much credit in the account of the death of Napoleon Bonaparte ... England and the un-holy alliance ... have drawn upon themselves the odium of the world." Though the *Gazette* prints a report of his funeral on September 5, the editors are still doubting reports of his death as late as September 10. It is not until October 15, under the heading of "Napoleon!!!" does the *Courier* finally solicit people to prepare a memorial for the fallen hero.

Imagine a plot was indeed conceived. Are we to believe, that around the beginning of October, 1821—a full five years and seven months after learning of Napoleon's incarceration—these crack sailors and ardent patriots were still not ready to sail? What took them so long? Even if the ship had to be specially built, it could not have taken 67 months to build it.

More legends revolve around Napoleon than just about any other figure in history. Without even looking at fabrications about his childhood, his romances, his soldiering, his innovations, and court intrigues, we could fill a book with fables around his exile. We find stories of pirates in Texas getting ready to nab him, and tales of his brothers putting up a ransom, or actually financing expeditions to rescue him. There are fantasies that he did, indeed, escape: to New York, to the swamps of Louisiana, back to Paris, to Italy to become a watchmaker. One odd incarnation has him as the secret brother of Jean Lafitte AND John Paul Jones!

Additionally, there are several buildings in the United States that claim to have been built for Napoleon's respite after being sprung from prison. Among the more famous were the *Beverly*, a lovely home that has since burned at King's Creek, Maryland; and the *Cup and Saucer House*, which was destroyed by fire in 1867 at Cape Vincent, New York. In every case of these homes, The Plot was a certainty, it involved famous historical figures, and Napoleon's death foiled the attempts.

Of course, his rescue must have been discussed, not only in New Orleans, but anywhere he had sympathizers. Further, there would have been, at any given time on the Mississippi River, a few tars who had actually been to St. Helena. Naturally, these roustabouts would plan a rescue in great detail. It is human nature, especially in bars, to endow one's self with a few extra fine qualities—one need only to watch a football game in a public place to hear how many expert coaches there are in the world. Imagine the heroes that walked the muddy streets of the Crescent City at the time of the exile, and imagine how many more appeared after Napoleon's death obviated any actual proof of that heroism.

The stories of The Plot first appear in print in the late nineteenth century. In Deléry's 1972 history, she reasonably surmises that New Orleans, freshly defeated in the Civil War, needed some sort of return to its former prestige. It is also at this time that the true French Creoles are dying out and the city is becoming less European. The French Quarter is becoming a slum. George Washington Cable and Lafcadio Hearn, almost in response, are creating their splendid portraits of the old city. Psychically, there had to be some connection with the former glory of *La République*. A story like this would be just the tonic.

Think of the political ramifications of such an enterprise. Assume the Creoles, now American citizens, were unafraid of any federal government reprisals. Further, it must be supposed the Frenchmen didn't care if they precipitated another war with England by liberating her worst enemy. They certainly must have thought about one of the things closest to their hearts: their wallets. A stunt like Napoleon's rescue would incur an acute financial loss by the city. Just a few months after the War of 1812 ended in New Orleans' own backyard, English merchant ships were starting to return to the city. The year 1815, logically and by many accounts, was a tough economic year for the city. It would take very little effort to figure out the loss in revenues from such an escapade. Perhaps, if there were a plan, this financial crunch caused the delay.

Perhaps, further, it is the discrepancies in time that caused local citizens to create the idea of the second house being built. Castellanos, in 1895, cites

Although Napoleon had his marriage to Josephine nullified in 1810 to marry Marie-Louise of Austria, his last word on his death bed was, "Josephine."

Picture of Empress Josephine in the second floor apartments of the Napoleon House

A window of the Hotel Ste. Helene next door to the Napoleon House.

a certain Mr. Lewis as the expert who knew of the plot. This Mr. Lewis possessed a clock that was to have been the Emperor's, had he come. It is easy to imagine much "imperial" bric-a-brac on the mantels of the city's living rooms. This would provide another impetus to asserting the story. The Dufilho Home at 514 Chartres, the present-day Pharmacy Museum, was indeed built close to the time of Napoleon's death. Only, Girod didn't build it. And sad to say for the ancient forebears of the *Antiques Roadshow*, when construction did begin in 1822, Bonaparte's passing was well known.

Nine characteristics define an urban legend:
- It is a narrative.
- Its veracity is questionable.
- It is alleged to be true.
- It is plausible enough to be believed.
- It is of indeterminate origin.
- It varies in the telling.
- It is attributed to a putatively trustworthy secondhand source (e.g. "a friend of a friend").
- It is passed from individual to individual orally or in written form.
- It may take the form of a cautionary tale.

The story of Napoleon's rescue meets every criterion. That doesn't mean it isn't true. It only means The Plot is very definitely part of American folklore.

And unlike the ridiculous legends that still persist in New Orleans today —the Baroness Pontalba had rocky love affair with Andrew Jackson; Marie Laveau was a vicious, vengeful practitioner of the worst forms of Voodoo, etc.—The Plot has a sort of truth. There had to be a time, probably dozens, when, after several crystal carafes of wine, a staunch Frenchman staggered up and cried, "Let's go get him, boys!" And curses would be cursed, toasts would be toasted, plans would be planned, and after many cries of *Vive l'Empereur!* everyone would go home and sleep it off.

So when the story of Napoleon's failed rescue is shouted from a passing mule buggy, it is not so jarring to the historical purist. The Plot must have happened, at least for a few hours in the communal confines of ancient pubs not unlike the one that bears the name "Napoleon House" today. The truth is more interesting in New Orleans than anything any guide-writer could make up; and as this legend is sort of true, subscribing to a belief in it is forgivable.

I remember the first time I ever went there ... enjoying a passing thunderstorm over a bottle of wine and a fruit-and-cheese board. I fell for ... the quality of light, the mood and decor that somehow remind you of both Europe and the tropics at the same time. A travel guide I once read placed Napoleon House in the category of "Velveteen Rabbit ambience" —that benign neglect, that elegant decadence that characterizes what I loved about New Orleans.

—Philip Greene
Attorney, writer, historian,
and descendant of A. A. Peychaud

500 rue chartres

three centuries of history

When New Orleans was the Capital
of the Spanish Province of Lui-
siana.

1762 — 1803

This street bore the name

CALLE D SAN LUIS

The corner of St. Louis and Chartres Streets appears on all the earliest maps of the city. When Bienville laid out the city, he created a neat rectangle of streets literally on the banks of the Mississippi. At that time, the river came right up to where the sidewalks of today's Decatur Street run. King Louis XIV, the Sun King, had recently died, and the street names of the Quarter reflect the many different players who could have possibly acceded to the throne.

Bienville knew where his croissant was buttered, and he named everything in the area for bigwigs back home. Rue Chartres (pronounced "charters" by locals) is probably named for the King's nephew, the Duc de Chartres (unpronounceable by locals); and St. Louis is named for the patron saint of the of the infant Louis, soon to be King Louis XV, the Well Beloved.

On maps before 1731, a building appears on the lot, but not on the corner. In 1731, a corner building is shown. In the Lassus drawing of 1726, all the buildings had a simple style—single story, tall windows exposed to the river breeze, with a pitched roof and chimney. After 1755, mapmakers seemed to have tired of drawing buildings, so it is not clear if the same building survived until the end of the century. There was indeed a building on the property in the 1790s. It is pretty much agreed that this building was destroyed in the catastrophic French Quarter fire of December 8, 1794.

Four years later, on October 26, 1798, François Claude Girod, a merchant and trader, bought the property at an estate auction. Claude passed away in 1814 and left the property to his brother,

Mayor Nicholas Girod. On April 28, 1814, Girod legally possessed the property, and within the year, began building a grand home. According to the succession, there was a "(two) storied house ... and dependencies" on the property. Though some wonder if Nicholas built on the existing building, anyone familiar with European high-rises knows that the Continental protocol begins counting from the second floor, while Americans count from the ground floor. Thus the Napoleon House itself would have been thought of by Creoles as a "two-storied" house. There are many citations, written and anecdotal, that the mayor built himself a new house. For example, Creole-*extraordinaire* and friend of the king, Bernard Marigny, requests in 1816 that his new building has ornaments "in the style of the one on the new house of Mr. Girod," and pinpoints the very location.

The Girod House architect was probably Frenchman Hyacinthe Laclotte, though some think it may have been the ubiquitous Barthélémy Lafon. The sentimental favorite has to be Laclotte though, because earlier he had designed a spiral staircase and belvedere for the Cabildo that was never executed. One of the unique features of the Girod House is the spiral staircase leading to the cupola on the roof. Though the tower would be cer-

"Uncle Joe's" apartment on the second floor of the St. Louis Street side, the oldest section of the Napoleon House.

Right and previous spread: historic photographs of the Napoleon House from the collection of the Louisiana State Museum.

tainly handy to tradesman/importer Girod to espy ships coming in, one could imagine the rare addition of a belvedere to a private home as the final word of a passionate artist.

The new home was designed in a style that was quite popular in France at the time—a three-and-a-half story townhouse, with a place for business below and residences above. The floor-to-ceiling windows and galleries fronting on both streets are necessities in the tropical warmth of the city. The pitched roof had handmade thick slate tiles that only recently were replaced, and are actually available as souvenirs.

Girod's house is situated across the street from Pierre Maspero's, which at the time was a coffee house and had a library upstairs featuring maps and reference books. It seems likely that many New Orleans heroes went there, and Girod, as mayor, most certainly would have entertained in his own home the likes of Andrew Jackson, Jean Lafitte, Dominique You, and visiting international dignitaries.

Though he had no children, Nicholas's extended family remained in the house throughout most of the nineteenth century, until they dispersed or died out. At the beginning of the 1900s, different parties owned the building briefly, and eventually it became Labourdette's Grocery. In 1914, Joseph Impastato rented the building for $20 a month. He ran his own grocery, lived upstairs with his brothers and sisters, cery, lived upstairs with his brothers and sisters, and finally bought the property in 1920 for $14,000.

In the side room of the Italian market, Impastato opened a tavern which proved to be a favorite with river workers and local businessmen. In later interviews, "Uncle Joe" admits that he served whiskey during Prohibition. Also, the third floor served as apartments until well into the 1980s. In 1935, he had a melon and cream-colored Carrara marble floor laid in the main room, as well as the beautiful tile work entrance way proclaiming the place as "The Napoleon House." Incidentally, the artisan who placed the marble floor also designed a chess table at that time that still occupies the center of the main room. Joe lived to be 100 years old, but he had transferred the business to his brother Peter around World War II. After Peter's death, his son, (Joe's nephew) Sal took the business and bought the building. It remains in the family's hands to this day.

In 1970, the Girod house was placed on the National Register of Historic Places and is considered to be of international architectural and historic interest. Hurricane Katrina and the ensuing floods, power outages, and lootings, miraculously did no serious damage to the building. Today, in addition to fine wines and arcane cocktails, the Napoleon House serves gourmet food for lunch and dinner, and the second floor is a classic venue available for special events. As the third century of life dawns for the Girod House, it remains a living legend in a legendary town.

The small, octagonal cupola of the Napoleon House.

There are many reasons to love the Napoleon House, but to me the most important is that the clock stops when you step through its doors. I've popped in for a quick Sazerac and ended up missing an appointment three hours later. To sit there in the middle of the afternoon, sipping a Pimm's and pensively munching a muffuletta, is to live in a world without BlackBerries or iPods or wireless anythings; without plane reservations or sales calls or do-it-or-else deadlines or political blogs or gangsta rap or awards shows or baristas or intelligent design or reality TV ... or any of the rest of the horseshit that makes modern life such a vexation and a trial.

— Dave Wondrich
(wishing he was at the Napoleon House now)
Esquire's Drinks Correspondent

500 rue chartres

the people of its past and present

Above: Francesco A. and Cecile Locecero Impastato, 1905
Right: James Impastato's wife, Bianca. She was a nurse when
they met during World War I.

The true story of 500 rue Chartres is the story of two families that hopefully came to a strange and wonderful land to create a new life. It is in the fabric of the culture of the devout Creoles of the early city, and the desperate Sicilian immigrants of a later time, to keep a close family: living together, running the business together. These cultures also share a keen understanding of Christian generosity. The Girods and the Impastatos both took active roles in their communities as entrepreneurs, service-providers, philanthropists, and in some cases even public servants. These two pillars—a strong family and an evolved sense of community—provide precisely the reasons the home and the business of the Napoleon House thrive today.

Nicholas Girod (1747-1840)

Nicholas, born in a region of France called Savoy, came to America with his two brothers in the 1770s. In New Orleans, he helped his brother François Claude with a mercantile and importing business. They also owned some land. Nicholas became more and more involved with the inner workings of the city until he was elected the fifth mayor of the city in 1812. At that time, he and some partners had set up *syndics*—sort of an early-day savings and loan organization, to help people finance their homes and businesses. In 1814, he was re-elected mayor, defeating a popular judge.

When the frightening shadow of a British invasion paralyzed the city, Girod was instrumental in helping Colonel Andrew Jackson organize the locals into militias. New Orleans had only recently become an American possession, and there was little love lost between the proud Creoles and the earthy "Kaintucks" from upriver; but Jackson later commented on the bravery and co-operation of all the men and women of the city. Indeed, Girod fought at the Battle of New Orleans, thereby making him, in addition to his other achievements, a war hero.

Later in 1815, Girod had to step down from the mayoralty "to salvage his waning personal finances," but, interestingly, he remained active in business. Only three months after his retirement, his syndic repossessed the house at 824 Royal

Street, known as the Dejan House today. He eventually bought that house as well, and rented it out. In a few years, Girod returned to the Cabildo, New Orleans' early City Hall, as a city alderman. He also found time to be the church warden for the Saint Louis Cathedral.

When his next door neighbors, the Chesneaus, died, likely of yellow fever, he adopted their children and ran their household. At the time of his death, on September 1, 1840, Nicholas Girod left hundreds of thousands of dollars to friends and charities all over town. Sadly, he had no children, and legal entanglements over his estate and its debts eroded the sum and left very little for the inheritors.

An unattributed portrait of Nicholas Girod that hangs in the second floor apartments.

Giuseppe (Joseph) Impastato (1885-1985)

It cost 15-year-old Joe and his father Salvatore $30 each to cross the Atlantic with 1,300 other Sicilians in 1900. He came from a tiny town outside of Palermo called Cinisi, and as the oldest brother, it was his duty to accompany dad to forge a new life in a new country. He first got work in Greco's macaroni factory. At the end of his life, Joe's formula for longevity would be, "I eat pasta," but he was not long for the business of making it as a young man. He had worked his way up to manager and pulled down the astronomical sum of two dollars a day, when he realized, "I couldn't get nowhere for my $2 a day, so I figured to go in business for myself."

The willful young Joe rented the Girod House to open his own grocery, and he married Rosalie Giuffre to begin a 65-year marriage. In 1920, he bought the property outright for $14,000. He operated a grocery, served sandwiches, and opened the barroom. Feeling a need to create some pleasant ambience, and harboring a passion for opera, Joe brought his Victrola down from his upstairs residence, with some opera records to play for customers. Today, almost a century later, the opera and classic music background at the Napoleon House has become an inviolate tradition.

Right: Giuseppe (Joseph) Impastato

Giuseppi and Rose Impastato, 1916. "Uncle Joe's" wife Rose was his business partner when the Napoleon House was a grocery store. She handled all the finances and books.

Impastato's Grocery, early 20th century

Around World War II, Joe decided he had worked long enough, saying "I made what I got," and leased it for a few years to a group that ran the place as a bookie joint and dance hall. After the war, his brother Peter took the reins. "Uncle Joe," or "Mr. Joe," as anyone meeting him, family or friend, would call him, remained at the house, living upstairs. As a new public interest in the charms of the Vieux Carré burgeoned, more and more visitors came and discovered the Napoleon House. By the time the building was declared a Historic Place in 1970, Joe had become a sort of landmark himself. Daily he would come downstairs and sit in the main room with his blossoming white eyebrows and a ready story for anyone who asked.

In his last year, 1985, he marked his one-hundredth birthday surrounded by 400 friends and family. Luminaries such as President Ronald Reagan and Pope John Paul II sent their felicitations. Joe Impastato celebrated a great life in a great way—among those who loved him, in his own home, which had become a home for many, many more.

Peter Impastato

Peter Impastato (1911-1971)

Salvatore Impastato, the father who brought Joe over in 1900, would have six children in all, four of them sons. Joseph and Peter would run the family business, but the other two sons followed acutely different directions. At one edge, Sam Impastato did not appreciate the vigor with which his oldest brother, Joseph, took charge in the new café. After a particularly violent demonstration of who was in charge, Sam scooped some cash out of the register and ran away to New York. At 14 he began to box. Though he returned to New Orleans, Sam never left boxing. He chose the name Tommie Littleton as his *nom-de-guerre* and eventually moved to Mobile to become an athletic trainer.

At the other edge, James Impastato led a life of almost incredible piety. As a *tertiary*, a kind of lay affiliate to the Catholic Church, James held dozens of offices, knighthoods, and certifications. His faithfulness was internationally acclaimed as he sat on boards of orphanages, relief agencies, and church councils. With the same sort of dedication demonstrated by his brothers in their chosen fields, James was remembered by the local papers as "one of the best loved and most outstanding lay leaders in New Orleans."

And at the center of this triangle formed by Joseph's drive for business, Sam's unbridled need for self-expression, and James' unbounded faith, sat Peter Impastato. Gentle and soft-spoken, Peter virtually took over the Napoleon House out a sense of familial duty. He was born in New Orleans and attended college at Spring Hill in Mobile. He married Tannie

James Impastato

Samaritano, then served in the United States Army for the Second World War, and when he returned to New Orleans, Joseph had offered the business to him.

Joe had lost interest in the business before the war, and the house was leased out for a few years to a group that catered to a slightly gruffer clientele. Perhaps because his own family was growing, four girls and a boy, Peter endeavored to re-establish the Napoleon House as a neighborhood bar. Like a lot of families in the 1950s, Peter's had moved out of the downtown area to a section called Gentilly. Every morning, he would take the public bus down Gentilly Boulevard, stop at the French Market to pick up the day's needs, and walk up to work.

Left: Peter Impastato
Right: James Impastato's son Salvatore, Peter Impastato's daughter Fara, and Sam Impastato's son Philip

The non-smoking, non-drinking barkeep soon achieved his desire for respectability of his establishment and more. A writer for the States-Item declared, "I have been in bars from Bourbon Street to Bombay, and never met a publican like Peter. He was curiously a stand-out sort of guy, which is paradoxical, because he was probably the most low-profile bar owner who ever poured a drink."

In many needy folks' minds, however, Peter was not low-profile. He not only freely gave to most groups that asked for help; he personally checked up on the sick, gave beds to the homeless, and shoved a few bucks into the pockets of stranded travellers. The accounts of his charity are legion, one of the most telling recounts his church membership. Though he actively belonged to Saint Leo's Church in Gentilly, he also served as lector at Saint Augustine Church in the Tremé neighborhood, because he wanted to help the then-poorer parish.

One gets the idea that Peter never felt entirely comfortable running a bar. "My dad never did want the kids to be involved with the business," his son Sal admits today. He even contemplated leasing out the building in the late 1960s. At the same time, he couldn't apply himself entirely to charitable service. "Pete would be happier to open one day a week and close down the other six," a customer recalled. "He'd have that much more time to visit friends in the hospital, bring food to the poor, and more time to spend with those who look to him for clothing and shelter."

With the senectitude of the Girod House gaining in reputability, and the vision of Joseph providing the French Quarter with a stylish

'Mr. Joe' celebrates life at 100

By JOAN KENT
Staff writer

Giuseppe Impastato, who has owned the Napoleon House since 1916, began Sunday the same way his nephew says he begins every day.

He sat at the kitchen table of his apartment above the French Quarter bar, said his prayers and drank a cup of coffee with a shot of Wild Turkey.

The rest of the day was different: "Mr. Joe" celebrated his 100th birthday.

The front door of the bar at Chartres and St. Louis streets was locked but inside the two rooms and patio were packed with about 400 friends and relatives. There were lots of babies, lots of little girls in party dresses and boys in suits, and lots of food and champagne. Framed congratulations from President Reagan, Mayor Dutch Morial and Congresswoman Lindy Boggs and a benediction from the Pope John Paul II on the occasion hung on the walls.

Mr. Joe sat quietly next to a table that held three cakes decorated with "Happy Birthday Mr. Joe," blue and white rosettes and six candles.

He held his cane, accepted greetings, smiled as everybody sang a rousing "Happy Birthday" and then walked over and blew out the six candles without the

Giuseppe Impastato proudly cuts his 100th birthday cake.
STAFF PHOTO BY NORMAN J. BERTEAUX JR.

slightest difficulty.

The Napoleon House, where people talk, play chess and listen to classical music on a record player in the back room, has been declared a Historical Landmark.

It was built in 1797. The building is said to have been offered to Napoleon in a plot to rescue him from exile on the island of Elba,

See MR. JOE, next page

Newspaper clipping from the family scrapbook, Times Picayune States Item, 1985.

service, there is no doubt that it was Peter's compassion and genteel approach that cultivated an environment of welcome and peace. A year before Peter passed away, the building was placed on the National Register of Historic Places; but even more important to Peter, one can be sure, the Napoleon House by that time was accepted into the hearts of a public that he worked so hard to serve.

Joe and nephew Sal Impastato

Back in 1973, Peter's son, Salvatore, took over the Napoleon House before he had reached the age of 24. Today, the family business is still in the family. Along with Sal and his wife, Vivian, his sisters Maria Impastato and Janie Lala, and his brother-in-law, Leonard Lala, every facet of the operation is in the hands of relatives.

And the fourth generation, 35-year-old Nicholas Impastato, Sal's son, stands ready to bring the Napoleon House into its next hundred years. Of course, the future is not without its challenges. Hurricane Katrina struck a devastating blow to the city's economy and collective psyche; but just weeks after the storm, the Impastato family was diligently on the job getting the place up and running, making it one of the first restaurant bars open in the post-disaster city.

As New Orleans continues its slow and uncertain comeback, the one certainty will be the Napoleon House's presence at her heart.

Nicholas Impastato

Dinner that night was the closest I've come to truly picturing myself in another time, when culture is so palpable. But in the case of the Napoleon House, it really was tangible.

—Taylor Rau
Editor, Nightclub & Bar Magazine
Oxford, Mississippi

food
the Napoleon House's signature dishes

Creole Jambalaya

Creole Jambalaya

- ½ stick butter
  - 1 pound Andouille or other spicy smoked sausage
  - ½ pound cooked chicken, diced

Melt butter and add sausage and chicken. Sauté for a few minutes.

- 3 medium onions, chopped
- 6 green onions with tops, chopped
- 1 small green bell pepper, chopped

Add onions and green pepper and sauté a few more minutes.

- 2 pounds small raw peeled shrimp
- 2 cups raw rice
- 2 cans (12 ounces each) beef broth
  or 3 cups beef bouillon
- 2 14½-ounce cans stewed tomatoes
- 4 cloves garlic, minced
- 1 bay leaf
- ½ teaspoon thyme
- ¼ teaspoon ground cumin
- ¼ teaspoon allspice
- ¼ teaspoon cayenne (optional)
- salt and pepper to taste

Add rest of ingredients and mix thoroughly.

Let the mixture come to a boil, then cover and cook over low heat until liquid is absorbed and rice is tender (about 30 minutes).

Serves 6.

Seafood Gumbo

- 3 pounds medium size shrimp, peeled
- 1 pint water
- 1 tsp. salt

Put shrimp in 1 pint water with salt and cook over medium heat about 5 minutes or until shrimp turns pink. Turn off heat, cover and let sit for 3 minutes. Drain, reserving liquid.

- 8 tablespoons vegetable oil
- 8 tablespoons all-purpose flour

In a large heavy pot, make a roux with oil and flour, as follows: Heat oil until hot. (Check by adding a pinch of flour to oil. If it sizzles, it is hot enough.) Add rest of flour and stir constantly until a deep golden brown. Be careful not to burn.

- 2 medium onions, chopped
- 1 small bell pepper, diced
- 2 sticks celery, chopped
- 4 toes garlic, diced
- 4 tablespoons green onion, chopped

Add onion, bell pepper, celery, garlic and green onion and sauté about 5 minutes.

- 2 pounds okra, cut in small pieces
- 2 cups chopped tomatoes, or canned stewed tomatoes
- 2 bay leaves
- 2 tablespoons parsley, chopped
- 6 pints water, including the shrimp broth
- ½ tablespoon Tony Chachere's Creole Seasoning

Add the rest of the ingredients except shrimp and crab meat. Bring to a boil, reduce heat, cover and simmer for 1 hour.

- 1 pound crab meat

Add shrimp and crab meat and simmer 30 minutes more. Serve over hot rice.

Serves 6.

Italian Olive Salad for Muffuletta

Chop and place in a large bowl:

- 1 cup pimiento-stuffed queen olives, chopped
- ⅓ cup canned artichoke hearts, drained and coarsely chopped
- ½ cup canned chickpeas, drained and coarsely chopped
- ¼ cup cocktail onions, drained and coarsely chopped
- ½ cup pickled vegetables, drained and coarsely chopped
- 1 tablespoon capers, drained
- ¼ cup green pepper, finely chopped
- ½ teaspoon garlic, minced

Add the following ingredients and mix well:

- ¼ cup extra virgin olive oil
- 2 tablespoons red wine vinegar
- 1 teaspoon dried oregano
- ½ teaspoon black pepper

Cover and refrigerate for at least 8 hours. May be stored in refrigerator for a week.

Yield: 3 cups

Napoleon House Muffuletta

Preheat oven to 350°.

- 1 9-inch seeded muffuletta bun or Italian seeded bread

Brush bottom and top halves of bun lightly with olive oil.

- 4 slices ham (about 4 ounces)
- 5 slices Genoa salami (about 2 ounces)
- 2 slices pastrami (about 2 ounces)
- 3 slices provolone cheese (about 2 ounces)
- 3 slices swiss cheese (about 2 ounces)

Layer on bottom half of bun.

- ⅔ cup Italian olive salad (see opposite page)

Top with olive salad and other half of bun.

Wrap in foil and bake for 20 minutes or until sandwich is thoroughly heated.

Makes one 9-inch sandwich.
(May be served in halves or quarters, as needed.)

Local color note: While the correct Italian pronunciation of this sandwich is something like "moo-foo-LEHT-tah," many local natives have adopted something more like "moo-fuh-LOTT-uh." Others just order a "muff."

Napoleon House Bruschetta

Preheat oven to 350°.

- 1 loaf braided Italian bread
- ¼ cup olive oil

Slice the bread in half lengthwise and brush both halves with olive oil.

- 4 tablespoons chopped garlic
- 1 cup shredded mozzarella cheese

Sprinkle chopped garlic and half of the mozzarella evenly over each piece.

- 2 ripe Roma tomatoes

Slice tomatoes crosswise into even circles and divide equally between the halves. Place bread halves face up on a baking sheet and bake for 10 to 15 minutes.

- ½ cup pesto (recipe below)
- ½ cup finely grated Parmesan cheese

Remove from oven and drizzle pesto, to taste, over each half. Sprinkle with Parmesan cheese. Slice into finger-size slices and serve.

Serves 4.

Pesto Sauce

- 1 pound fresh basil leaves, stems removed
- 4 cups extra-virgin olive oil
- ¼ cup fresh lemon juice
- 2 tablespoons fresh garlic, minced
- 1 tablespoon kosher salt
- 1 tablespoon black pepper

Place olive oil into blender, then add all of the other ingredients.

Puree until smooth. Refrigerate.

Makes 5 cups.

Red Beans

Napoleon House Red Beans

- 1 pound dried red (kidney) beans
- ½ cup diced yellow onion
- 1 rib celery, diced
- 4 cloves garlic, finely chopped
- 4 sprigs fresh chopped parsley, or ¼ cup dried
- 1 green bell pepper, diced
- 1 pound smoked sausage
- 1 ham bone (optional)
- 1 or 2 bay leaves
- ½ teaspoon thyme
- Salt and pepper to taste
- Chicken base (optional)

Place all ingredients in a large, heavy-bottomed pot.

Fill pot with plain water or water with chicken base (this already contains salt), to two inches above the ingredients.

Bring to boil and then reduce to a simmer, cover and cook over low heat for 2½ to 3 hours.

Serve over prepared white rice.

Serves 8.

Napoleon House Remoulade Sauce

- 4 or 5 hard-boiled eggs, cooled

Peel and separate eggs. Dice yolks very fine. Puree or finely dice whites. Set aside.

- ½ cup Creole mustard
- 1 tablespoon horseradish
- 4 or 5 large egg yolks*, beaten until bright yellow
- 2 cups canola oil
- 2 tablespoon + 1 tsp ketchup
- 1 tablespoon + ½ teaspoon paprika
- ⅛ teaspoon garlic powder
- ½ teaspoon salt

In a large bowl combine creole mustard and horseradish.

Beat egg yolks until bright yellow and add to mustard mixture. Whisk until incorporated. Slowly whisk in half the canola oil, adding it in a thin stream. Whisk constantly until emulsified.

Add ketchup, paprika and garlic powder.

Whisk in remaining oil in a thin stream until emulsified.

Add chopped boiled egg yolks and egg whites and mix well. Add salt.

Cover and refrigerate until ready to use. Keep refrigerated and use within 2-3 days.

Serve with boiled or sautéed shrimp, cooked rice, and fresh tomato over romaine leaves. Garnish with sliced purple onions.

Yield: 12 servings (¼ cup each)

*Use only pasteurized eggs when preparing a recipe that calls for raw eggs.

The Napoleon House is wonderfully ancient, delightfully dark, with the alluring smell and patina that comes with age; the only apparent change to the place is the change of clothing and hairstyles on the patrons who now come to the Napoleon House to drink Pimm's Cups, their house specialty drink.

—Debra C. Argen
Editor in Chief
Luxury Experience Magazine

drinks

classic New Orleans cocktails from the classic New Orleans bar

Napoleon House bartender Greg Cowman.

Pimm's Cup

- 1½ ounces Pimm's Original No. 1
- about 3 ounces pure lemon juice
- 7-UP
- a slice of cucumber for garnish

Fill a tall, slender glass with ice. Pour in the Pimm's and lemon juice. Add 7-UP to fill.

Garnish with cucumber slice.

Mint Julep

Mint Julep

- 4 springs fresh mint
- 2½ ounces bourbon
- 1 teaspoon sugar
- 2 teaspoons water
- additional mint leaves for garnish

Muddle mint leaves, sugar and water in a tall glass.
Fill glass with crushed ice and add bourbon.

Garnish with extra mint leaves.

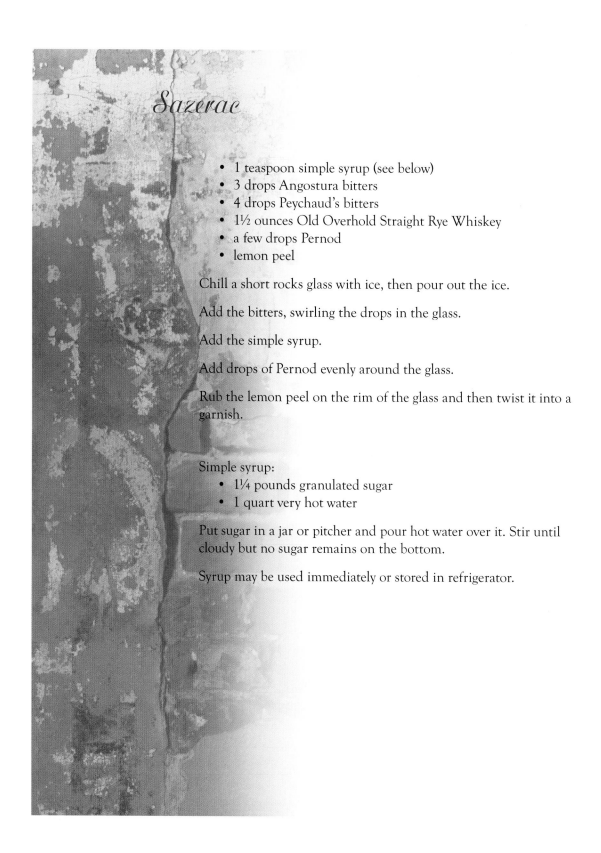

Sazerac

- 1 teaspoon simple syrup (see below)
- 3 drops Angostura bitters
- 4 drops Peychaud's bitters
- 1½ ounces Old Overhold Straight Rye Whiskey
- a few drops Pernod
- lemon peel

Chill a short rocks glass with ice, then pour out the ice.

Add the bitters, swirling the drops in the glass.

Add the simple syrup.

Add drops of Pernod evenly around the glass.

Rub the lemon peel on the rim of the glass and then twist it into a garnish.

Simple syrup:
- 1¼ pounds granulated sugar
- 1 quart very hot water

Put sugar in a jar or pitcher and pour hot water over it. Stir until cloudy but no sugar remains on the bottom.

Syrup may be used immediately or stored in refrigerator.

Cajun Mary

Cajun Mary

- ½ teaspoon horseradish
- 2 teaspoons Lea & Perrins Worcestershire Sauce
- 1 teaspoons Louisiana Hot Sauce
- ½ teaspoon celery salt
- 3 or 4 dashes black pepper
- 2 ounces Absolut Peppar vodka
- 4 ounces V-8 juice

Pour all ingredients into a shaker, shake well, and pour.

Top with a jalapeño, pickled okra, fresh lime and lemon and spiced beans.

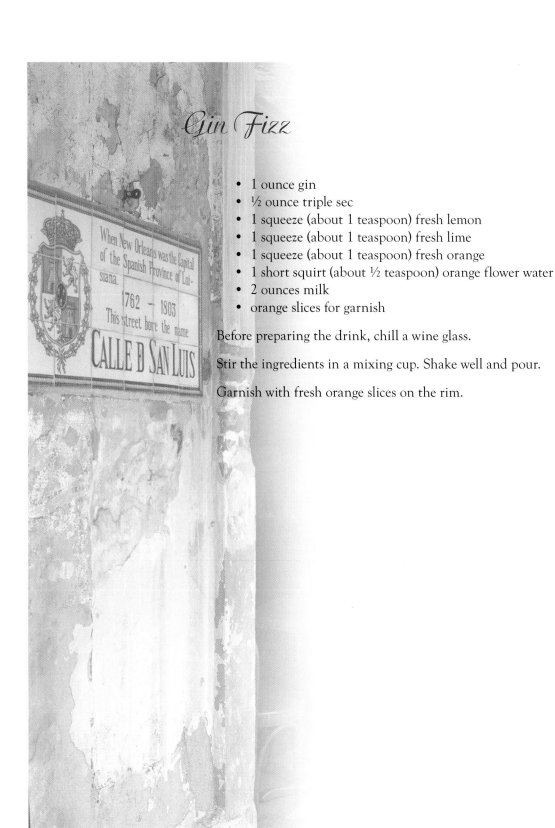

Gin Fizz

- 1 ounce gin
- ½ ounce triple sec
- 1 squeeze (about 1 teaspoon) fresh lemon
- 1 squeeze (about 1 teaspoon) fresh lime
- 1 squeeze (about 1 teaspoon) fresh orange
- 1 short squirt (about ½ teaspoon) orange flower water
- 2 ounces milk
- orange slices for garnish

Before preparing the drink, chill a wine glass.

Stir the ingredients in a mixing cup. Shake well and pour.

Garnish with fresh orange slices on the rim.

Gin Fizz

Planter's Punch

Planter's Punch

- 1 ounce white rum
- 1½ ounces lemon juice
- 1½ ounces orange juice
- 1½ ounces cranberry juice
- 1½ ounces pineapple juice
- 2 dashes grenadine

Fill a tall, slender glass with ice.

In a separate glass, mix white rum, juices and grenadine well and pour over ice.

- 1 orange slice
- 1 cherry
- 1 ounce Myers rum

Add orange slice and cherry to glass. Pour Myers rum on top.

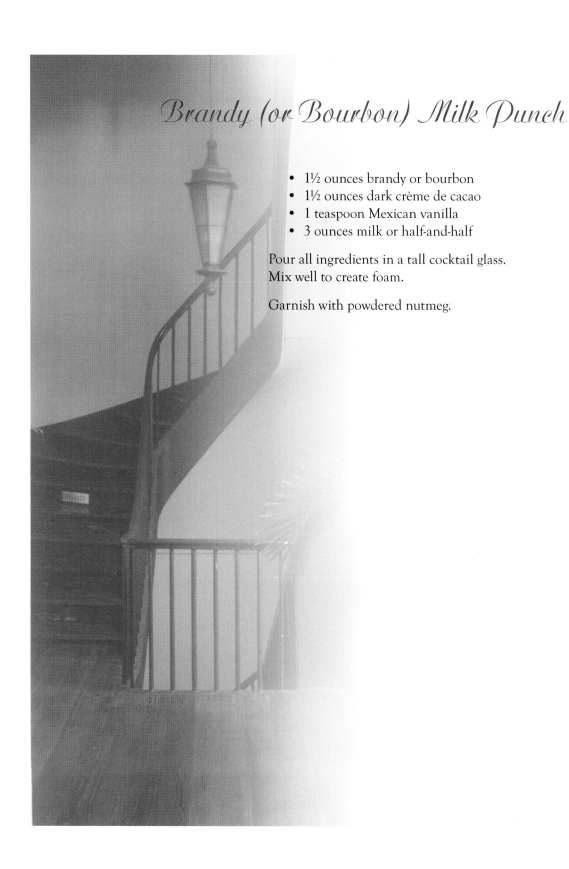

Brandy (or Bourbon) Milk Punch

- 1½ ounces brandy or bourbon
- 1½ ounces dark crème de cacao
- 1 teaspoon Mexican vanilla
- 3 ounces milk or half-and-half

Pour all ingredients in a tall cocktail glass.
Mix well to create foam.

Garnish with powdered nutmeg.

Brandy Milk Punch

Grasshopper

Grasshopper

- 1½ ounces crème de menthe
- 1½ ounces crème de cacao
- 3 ounces milk

Chill a 6-ounce wine glass.

Pour the crème de menthe, crème de cacao and milk into a shaker. Shake well and pour into chilled glass.

The past is never dead; it's not even past.

— William Faulkner

Bibliography

Essential Books

Arthur, Stanley Clisby. *Old New Orleans*. New Orleans, Harmanson: 1936.
Caillot, Pierre. "Relation du Voyage de la Louisianne ou Nouvelle France." Handwritten manuscript. 1730.
Castellanos, Henry C. *New Orleans As It Was*. New Orleans: 1895.
Coleman, Will H. *Historical Sketchbook and Guide to New Orleans*. New Orleans: 1885.
Conrad, Glenn R., ed. *A Dictionary of Louisiana Biography*. New Orleans, La Historical Assn: 1988.
Gayarré, Charles. *Histoire de la Louisiane*. New Orleans: 1866. English version, New Orleans: 1903.
McCaffety, Kerri. *Obituary Cocktail: The Great Saloons of New Orleans*. New Orleans: Vissi d'Arte Books, 2001.
de la Souchère Deléry, Simone. *Napoleon's Soldiers in Louisiana*. New Orleans: Pelican, 1972.
Twain, Mark. *Life on the Mississippi*. New York: 1883. New York: Penguin Classics, 1986.

Additionally, no research on any aspect of the French Quarter can ignore the voluminous study conducted in 1966 found in the Vieux Carré Survey housed at the Williams Research Center of The Historic New Orleans Collection:

The Historic New Orleans Collection. *Vieux Carré Survey, Squares 27, 27 w/Maps, and 47*. New Orleans: 1966.
The Historic New Orleans Collection. *Map Book. Compilation of City Maps 1720-1966*.

Selected Articles

An exhaustive catalog of articles written on the Napoleon House in worldwide newspapers, journals, magazines and tour books, assuming one could possibly be compiled, is beyond the scope of this work. With few wonderful exceptions, most articles written on the Napoleon House focus on the things in which the tourist might be interested: the unique ambience, the great food, the Napoleon rescue plot, and the Pimm's Cup. Some of the articles cited here are in the possession of the Impastato family, as they are deemed worth preserving, it makes a fine criterion for their selection.

AirFare, Jul 1991. (Ohio State publication) A story on "The Plot."
Clarion Herald, Aug 21, 1969. Mel Leavitt. "Toasting to Napoleon." The building of the house.
Clarion Herald, Nov 18, 1971. "An Atomic Age St. Vincent." The inspiring charity of Peter Impastato.
Daily Picayune, Jun 16, 1907. Thomas Ewing Dabney. "The True Story of Napoleon's House." Borrowing copiously from Castellanos and Coleman, luridly recounts "The Plot," and claims that 514 Chartres is the real Imperial house.
Dixie (Times-Picayune supplement), Sep 20, 1981. Millie Ball. "Joseph Impastato, Emperor of the Napoleon House." Excellent feature on the venerable founder of the Napoleon House.
Dixie (Times-Picayune supplement), Mar 2, 1986. Ronnie Virgets. "Dropping by the Napoleon House." Portrait of the people and ambience, by one of New Orleans' greatest all-time chroniclers.
Esquire Guide to the Bars, 1982. A piece on the belvedere, "The Plot," and the Pimm's Cup.
Food and Wine, Aug 1992. Great bartenders of America - Napoleon House's own Gregory Cowman.

Inter Nos, (monthly bulletin for The Third Order, Cincinnati), Feb, 1962. Feature on the devout life of Joe's brother, James Impastato, Knight of Saint Gregory.

Italian-American Digest (New Orleans), Fall, 1982. Mike Palao. History of Joe Impastato at the Napoleon House.

Lagniappe (States-Item supplement), Aug 2, 1975. Five French Quarter elders (including Joe Impastato) reminisce about old New Orleans.

National Geographic Traveler, Spring 1987. New Orleans feature.

Neuroscientist Society Annual Meeting, 1987. Convention guide. Travel suggestions.

New Orleans Magazine, Dec 1995. Best of New Orleans selection.

New Orleans Magazine, June 1996. Marc Cooper, Vieux Carré Commission director, talks about his favorite place.

New Orleans Magazine, Dec 1998. New Orleans bar feature.

New Orleans Magazine, July 1999. Napoleon House inspired photographer Kerri McCaffety to write Obituary Cocktail.

New Orleans Magazine, Aug 1999. Short piece.

New York Press, Dec 6, 1999. Joseph Bonaparte finances rescue mission for his brother.

Southern Accents, Jan-Feb 1999. The Pimm's Cup.

States, Aug 8, 1953. "N.O. Houses." Thorough review of history and architecture of the Girod House.

States-Item, Oct 9, 1963. Louis J. Dufilho, Jr. built 514 Chartres (today's Pharmacy Museum) in 1823.

States-Item, Dec 4, 1971. Clint Bolton. "Pete's Napoleon House." A moving memorial to Peter Impastato.

States-Item, Jun 6, 1973. Pepe Citron. "Great Bars in N.O." Error-filled story with a good interview of Sal Impastato and an overview of the waitstaff.

States-Item, Jun 6, 1977. Jim Amoss. A masterfully written look at the immigration of Joe Impastato and 1,300 other Sicilians to New Orleans by the future editor of the Times Picayune States Item.

Times Picayune States Item, Jul 29, 1985. Joan Kent. "'Mr. Joe' celebrates life at 100." Joe Impastato's 100th birthday party.

Times Picayune States Item, Jan 28, 1990. Marjorie Roehl. History based on Coleman.

Tulanian, Summer, 2001. Roy Hoffman. "Tommie Littleton: Gentleman Boxer." Outlines the odyssey of Sam Impastato (Joe's younger brother) as a runaway-turned-professional boxer.

TWA Ambassador, Jan 1987. Used to lead a feature on New Orleans.

USA Today, Dec 20, 2005. The comeback of New Orleans after Hurricane Katrina with quote from Maria, Sal Impastato's sister.

Vieux Carré Courier, Feb 19, 1965. Edith Elliot Long. Charming discussion of the Girod House architecture.

Vieux Carré Courier, May 30, 1969. Edith Elliot Long. Histories of the houses along St. Louis Street, adjoining Napoleon House.

Vieux Carré Courier, Oct 31, & Nov 9, 1969. Locals protest Napoleon House remodeling and leasing.

Vieux Carré Courier, Jun 5, 1970. "Living Landmark." Girod House becomes a National Historical Landmark.

Where Magazine, Dec 31 1983. History of the Impastato family, "The Plot," and the Pimm's Cup.

Bibliography

New Orleans Newspapers
Clarion Herald, selected articles 1969 - 2002.
Louisiana Courier, 1814-1822.
Louisiana Gazette, 1814-1822.
New Orleans States, selected articles.
New Orleans States-Item, selected articles.
New Orleans Daily Picayune, selected articles.
New Orleans Times Picayune States Item, selected articles.

Websites
A search on Google for "Napoleon House" will bring back 12,000,000 websites. Like most subjects online, the sites range from the inspiringly executed to the interplanetarily conceived. The following were used in some way in the research of this book.

Architecture
http://www.neworleansonline.com/archive/arch-vieuxcarre.shtml - Enjoyable overview of the houses of New Orleans.
The Bonapartes in America
http://rumskulls.org/1800s.html - Napoleon coming to live in Maryland due to his brother Jerome.
http://www.marylandhistoricaltrust.net/nr/NRDetail.asp?HDID=137&FROM=NRMapSO.html - The Beverly, a home in Maryland reputedly set to entertain Napoleon.
http://www.rootsweb.com/~nyjeffer/tid27.htm - Cup and Saucer House in New York was built for Napoleon.
http://www.findarticles.com/p/articles/mi_m1026/is_4_162/ai_92545137 - Joseph Bonaparte's home in New Jersey.
Mayor Girod
http://nutrias.org/~nopl/info/louinfo/admins/girod.htm - The peerless New Orleans Public Library research site.
http://www.enlou.com/no_people/girodn-bio.htm - The easily accessible Encyclopedia Louisiana.
Pirates, 19th Century Life
http://www.cindyvallar.com/NewOrleans.html - Pirates and an excellent New Orleans bibliography.
Plots to Free Napoleon
http://hirschey.homestead.com/watertown_history.html - Napoleon's older brother Joseph financed rescue effort.
http://web2.airmail.net/napoleon/IMPERIAL_GUARD_infantry_1.htm - Lafittes pirates in Texas planned a rescue.
http://www.dcmilitary.com/navy/seaservices/10_40/features/37480-1.html - A rescue of Napoleon was planned using a submarine designed by Robert Fulton.
http://pratie.blogspot.com/2005/02/jewish-pirates-save-louisiana.html - Jean Lafitte was Jewish, and his brother (sic) Dominique You would Captain "The Plot." (In reality, You was not related to Lafitte).
Urban Legends
http://urbanlegends.about.com/cs/urbanlegends/f/urbanlegends1.htm
http://www.snopes.com/info/ul-def.asp